MW01068031

Inspiration

&

Wisdom

from the Pen of

Ralph Waldo

Emerson

Compiled & edited
by
ODELIA FLORIS

Also by Odelia Floris

Nonfiction:
The Complete Poems of Ralph Waldo Emerson

Adult fiction:
The Heart of Darkness (The Chaucy Shire Medieval Mysteries Book 1)

Beguile Me Not

Children's fiction:
The Little Demon Who Couldn't

www.odeliafloris.com

Contents

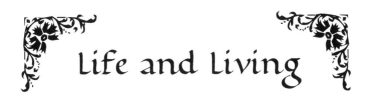

Life and Living

We are always getting ready to live, but never living.

When rats leave a sinking ship, where exactly do they think they are going?

Let us be poised, and wise, and our own, today.

Adopt the pace of nature. Her secret is patience.

That man is idle who can do something better.

No one can cheat you out of ultimate success but yourself.

For the most part only the light characters travel. Who are you that you have no task to keep you at home?

Make the most of yourself, for that is all there is of you.

Many might go to heaven with half the labor they go to hell.

One of the illusions of life is that the present hour is not the critical decisive hour. Write it on your heart that every day is the best day in the year. No man has learned anything rightly until he knows that every day is Doomsday.

For every benefit which you receive, a tax is levied.

To finish the moment, to find the journey's end in every step of the road, to live the greatest number of good hours, is wisdom.

Every calamity is a spur and valuable hint.

Cannot we please ourselves with performing our work, or gaining truth and power, without being praised for it?

Life is a perpetual instruction in cause and effect.

The whole of what we know is a system of compensations. Each suffering is rewarded; each sacrifice is made up; every debt is paid.

This time, like all times, is a very good one if we but know what to do with it.

Fate is nothing but the deeds committed in a prior state of existence.

The compensations of calamity are made apparent to the understanding also, after long intervals of time.

Commerce is of trivial import; love, faith, truth of character, the aspiration of man, these are sacred.

The reward of a thing well done, is to have done it.

We must set up a strong present tense against all rumors of wrath, past and to come.

Whatever course you decide upon, there is always someone to tell you that you are wrong. There are always difficulties arising which tempt you to believe that your critics are right. To map out a course of action and follow it to an end requires courage.

Every wall is a door.

Success comes from within, not from without.

If a man can write a better book, preach a better sermon or make a better mousetrap than his neighbors, though he build his house in the woods, the world will make a beaten path to his door.

Do not be too timid and squeamish about your actions. All life is an experience.

These times of ours are serious and full of calamity, but all times are essentially alike.

Today is a king in disguise.

Don't waste yourself in rejection, nor bark against the bad, but chant the beauty of the good.

To live without duties is obscene.

Let the stoics say what they please, we do not eat for the good of living, but because the meat is savory and the appetite is keen.

If we live truly we shall see truly.

Do what we can summer will have its flies.

There is no chance and no anarchy in the universe. All is system and gradation. Every god is there sitting in his sphere.

Finish each day and be done with it. You have done what you could. Some blunders and absurdities no doubt crept in; forget them as soon as you can. Tomorrow is a new day; begin it well and serenely and with too high a spirit to be encumbered with your old nonsense.

To be yourself in a world that is constantly trying to make you something else is the greatest accomplishment.

It is easy to live for others, everybody does. I call on you to live for yourself.
I wish that life should not be cheap, but sacred. I wish the days to be as centuries, loaded, fragrant.

Whatever limits us we call Fate.

By persisting in your path, though you forfeit the little you gain the great.

Life is a succession of lessons which must be lived to be understood.

Live in the sunshine, swim the sea, drink the wild air.

The days come and go like muffled and veiled figures, sent from a distant friendly party; but they say nothing, and if we do not use the gifts they bring, they carry them as silently away.

The prudence in life is concentration.

All are needed by each one; nothing is fair or good alone.

Most of the shadows of this life are caused by standing in one's own sunshine.

A man builds a fine house; and now he has a master and a task for life: he is to furnish, watch, show it and keep it in repair the rest of his days.

Be an opener of doors for such as come after thee.

No matter how often defeated, you are born to victory.

When a man is pushed, tormented, defeated, he has a chance to learn something.

How much of human life is lost in waiting.

I look on that man as happy who, when there is a question of success, looks into his work for a reply.
Solitude is impractical and yet society is fatal.

Shallow men believe in luck, believe in circumstances — it was somebody's name, or he happened to be there at the time, or it was so then, and another day would have been otherwise. Strong men believe in cause and effect.

The more experiments you make the better.

So nigh is grandeur to our dust, so near is God to man. When Duty whispers low, Thou must, the youth replies, I can.

So much of our time is spent in preparation, so much in routine and so much in retrospect, that the amount of each person's genius is confined to a very few hours.

Live, let live and help live.

For everything you have missed, you have gained something else, and for everything you gain, you lose something else.

The surest poison is time.

As the traveler who has lost his way throws his reins on his horse's neck and trusts to the instinct of the animal to find his road, so must we do with the divine animal who carries us through this world.

Difficulties exist to be surmounted.

The greatest gift is a portion of thyself.

It is one of the most beautiful compensations of life that no man can sincerely try to help another without helping himself.

It is not length of life but depth of life.

There are no days in life so memorable as those which vibrate to some stroke of the imagination.

We walk alone in the world.

As soon as there is life there is danger.

My angel — his name is Freedom — choose him to be your king. He shall cut pathways east and west, and fend you with his wing.

Make yourself necessary to somebody.

Life is not measured by the number of breaths we take, but by the moments that take our breath away.

All life is an experiment.

Nothing is beneath you if it is in the direction of your life.

Those who live to the future must always appear selfish to those who live to the present.

Envy is the tax which all distinction must pay.

My life is not an apology, but a life. It is for itself and not for a spectacle. I much prefer that it should be of a lower strain, so it be genuine and equal, than that it should be glittering and unsteady.

In skating over thin ice our safety is in our speed.

As soon as there is life there is danger.

Once you make a decision, the universe conspires to make it happen.

A good intention but fixed and resolute —
bent on high and holy ends, we shall find
means to them on every side and at every
moment; and even obstacles and opposition
will but make us "like the fabled specter-
ships," which sail the fastest in the very
teeth of the wind.

Our chief want in life is somebody who shall
make us do what we can.

Every sweet hath its sour, every evil its good.

It is very easy in the world to live by the
opinion of the world. It is very easy in
solitude to be self-centered. But the finished
man is he who in the midst of the crowd
keeps with perfect sweetness the
independence of solitude.

Be silly. Be honest. Be kind.

A person's life is limited but serving the
people is limitless. I want to devote my
limited life to serving the people limitlessly.

*The secrets of life are not shown except to
sympathy and likeness.*

Only so much do I know, as I have lived.

Without ambition one starts nothing. Without work one finishes nothing. The prize will not be sent to you; you have to win it.
Be not the slave of your own past—plunge into the sublime seas, dive deep, and swim far, so you shall come back with new self-respect, with new power, and with an advanced experience that shall explain and overlook the old.

Guard well your spare moments. They are like uncut diamonds. Discard them and their value will never be known, improve them and they will become the brightest gems in a useful life.

Hitch your wagon to a star. Let us not lag in paltry works which serve our pot and bag alone.

Love and Friendship

A friend may well be reckoned the masterpiece of nature.

Love is saying 'I feel differently' instead of 'You are wrong.'

I do with my friends as I do with my books. I would have them where I can find them, but I seldom use them.

The only way to have a friend is to be one.

A friend is someone who understands your past, believes in your future, and accepts you just the way you are.

A friend is a person with whom I may be sincere. Before him I may think aloud.

Love and you shall be loved. All love is mathematically just as much as the two sides of an algebraic equation.

A friend is a sane man who exercises not my ingenuity, but me.

It is one of the blessings of old friends that you can afford to be stupid with them.

Every man passes his life in the search after friendship.

A true friend is somebody who can make us do what we can.

He who has a thousand friends has not a friend to spare, and he who has one enemy will meet him everywhere.

My friends have come to me unsought. The good Lord gave them to me.

Go oft to the house of thy friend, for weeds choke the unused path.

Friends, such as we desire, are dreams and fables.

Friendship is an order of nobility; from its revelations we come more worthily into nature.

We talk of choosing our friends, but friends are self-elected.

The condition which high friendship demands is ability to do without it.

He who is in love is wise and is becoming wiser, sees newly every times he looks at the object beloved, drawing from it with his eyes and his mind those virtues which it possesses.

Thou art to me a delicious torment.

I do not wish to treat friendships daintily, but with roughest courage. When they are real, they are not glass threads or frost work, but the solidest things we can know.

A day for toil, an hour for sport, but for a friend is life too short.

Is not marriage an open question, when it is alleged, from the beginning of the world, that such as are in the institution wish to get out, and such as are out wish to get in?

The glory of friendship is not the outstretched hand, nor the kindly smile nor the joy of companionship; it is the spiritual inspiration that comes to one when he discovers that someone else believes in him and is willing to trust him.

The ornament of a house is the friends who frequent it.

A man's growth is seen in the successive choirs of his friends. For every friend whom he loses for truth, he gains a better.

Two may talk and one may hear, but three cannot take part in a conversation of the most sincere and searching sort.

Dear to us are those who love us, but dearer are those who reject us as unworthy, for they add another life; they build a heaven before us whereof we had not dreamed, and thereby supply to us new powers out of the recesses of the spirit, and urge us to new and unattempted performances.

Happy is the house that shelters a friend!

People

There is also this benefit in brag, that the speaker is unconsciously expressing his own ideal. Humor him by all means, draw it all out, and hold him to it.

People only see what they are prepared to see.

The louder he talked of his honor the faster we counted our spoons.

Who shall set a limit to the influence of a human being?

Wise men are not wise at all hours, and will speak five times from their taste or their humor to once from their reason.

Every man alone is sincere. At the entrance of a second person, hypocrisy begins.

Man is physically as well as metaphysically a thing of shreds and patches, borrowed unequally from good and bad ancestors, and a misfit from the start.

The good man has absolute good, which like fire turns every thing to its own nature, so that you cannot do him any harm.

Every man is an impossibility until he is born.

A man is a God in ruins.

The age of a woman doesn't mean a thing. The best tunes are played on the oldest fiddles.

Welcome evermore to gods and men is the self-helping man.

Don't say things. What you are stands over you the while, and thunders so that I cannot hear what you say to the contrary.

Fame is proof that people are gullible.

Where there is no vision a people perish.

All conservatives are such from personal defects. They have been effeminated by position or nature, born halt and blind through luxury of their parents and can only, like invalids, act on the defensive.

There is no one who does not exaggerate!

I hate the giving of the hand unless the whole man accompanies it.

Only an inventor knows how to borrow, and every man is or should be an inventor.

Things are in the saddle and ride mankind.

People wish to be settled. It is only as far as they are unsettled that there is any hope for them.

Men are conservatives when they are least vigorous or when they are most luxurious. They are conservatives after dinner or before taking their rest; when they are sick or aged. In the morning or when their intellect or their conscience has been aroused, when they hear music or when they read poetry, they are radicals.

Every man believes that he has greater possibilities.

As there is a use in medicine for poisons so the world cannot move without rogues.

The great majority of men are bundles of beginnings.

Nothing astonishes men so much as common sense and plain dealing.

Infancy conforms to nobody; all conform to it so that one babe commonly makes four or five out of the adults who prattle and play to it.

All sensible people are selfish, and nature is tugging at every contract to make the terms of it fair.

Everything runs to excess; every good quality is noxious if unmixed.

The power which resides in man is new in nature and none but he knows what that is which he can do, nor does he know until he has tried.

We do not count a man's years until he has nothing else to count.

One man's justice is another's injustice; one man's beauty is another's ugliness; one man's wisdom is another's folly.

The world is upheld by the veracity of good men: they make the earth wholesome.

And striving to be Man, the worm mounts through all the spires of form.

The masses have no habit of self-reliance or original action.

Masses are rude, lame, unmade, pernicious in their demands and influence, and need not to be flattered but to be schooled. I wish not to concede anything to them but to tame, drill, divide and break them up and draw individuals out of them.

If you would lift me up you must be on higher ground.

Trust men and they will be true to you; treat them greatly, and they will show themselves great.

A man is what he thinks about all day long.

Coolness and absence of heat and haste indicate fine qualities.

Nothing is more disgusting than the crowing about liberty by slaves, as most men are, and the flippant mistaking for freedom of some paper preamble like a Declaration of Independence or the statute right to vote by those who have never dared to think or to act.

Oh man! There is no planet, sun or star could hold you if you but knew what you are.

Few people have any next; they live from hand to mouth without a plan and are always at the end of their line.

In every man there is something wherein I may learn of him and in that I am his pupil.

No one has a prosperity so high and firm that two or three words can't dishearten it.

Men are respectable only as they respect.

The best efforts of a fine person are felt after we have left their presence.

People do not seem to see that their opinion of the world is also a confession of character.

The end of the human race will be that it will eventually die of civilization.

We must be as courteous to a man as we are to a picture, which we are willing to give the advantage of a good light.

Liberty is slow fruit. It is never cheap; it is made difficult because freedom is the accomplishment and perfectness of man.

The eyes indicate the antiquity of the soul.

Men lose their tempers in defending their taste.

Gross and obscure natures, however decorated, seem impure shambles; but character gives splendor to youth and awe to wrinkled skin and gray hairs.

As long as a man stands in his own way everything seems to be in his way.

The perception of the comic is a tie of sympathy with other men, a pledge of sanity and a protection from those perverse tendencies and gloomy insanities in which fine intellects sometimes lose themselves. A rogue alive to the ludicrous is still convertible. If that sense is lost, his fellow-men can do little for him.

Men cease to interest us when we find their limitations.

When the eyes say one thing and the tongue another, a practiced man relies on the language of the first.

He who would be a man must therefore be a non-conformist.

The mob is man voluntarily descending to the nature of the beast.

A man must consider what a rich realm he abdicates when he becomes a conformist.

The intellectual man requires a fine bait; the sots are easily amused. But everybody is drugged with his own frenzy and the pageant marches at all hours with music and banner and badge.

No member of a crew is praised for the rugged individuality of his rowing.

We all boil at different degrees.

There is no strong performance without a little fanaticism in the performer.

A man's personal defects will commonly have with the rest of the world precisely that importance which they have to himself. If he makes light of them, so will other men.

The foundations of a person are not in matter but in spirit.

Let us treat the men and women well; treat them as if they were real; perhaps they are.

A man finds room in the few square inches of the face for the traits of all his ancestors; for the expression of all his history and his wants.

In conversation the game is to say something new with old words. And you shall observe a man of the people picking his way along step by step, using every time an old boulder yet never setting his foot on an old place.

No change of circumstances can repair a defect of character.

Great men or men of great gifts you shall easily find, but symmetrical men never.

For what are they all in their high conceit, when man in the bush with God may meet?

Every book is a quotation; and every house is a quotation out of all forests and mines and stone quarries; and every man is a quotation from all his ancestors

A cynic can chill and dishearten with a single word.

Intellect annuls fate. So far as a man thinks, he is free.

If a man knew anything he would he would sit in a corner and be modest; but he is such an ignorant peacock that he goes bustling up and down and hits on extraordinary discoveries.

We do not quite forgive a giver. The hand that feeds us is in some danger of being bitten.

If a man owns land, the land owns him.

There are many things of which a wise man might wish to be ignorant

A man in debt is so far a slave.

An eye can threaten like a loaded and leveled gun, or it can insult like hissing or kicking; or, in its altered mood, by beams of kindness, it can make the heart dance for joy.

Sanity is very rare. Every man almost, and every woman, has a dash of madness.

There is always room for a person of force, and they make room for many.

My evening visitors, if they cannot see the clock, should find the time in my face.

The greatest difficulty is that men do not think enough of themselves, do not consider what it is that they are sacrificing when they follow in a herd, or when they cater for their establishment.

A man is the whole encyclopedia of facts. The creation of a thousand forests is in one acorn, and Egypt, Greece, Rome, Gaul, Britain, America, lie folded already in the first man.

The people are to be taken in very small doses.

What is a man born for but to be a reformer, a remaker of what has been made, a denouncer of lies, a restorer of truth and good?

It is impossible for a man to be cheated by anyone but himself.

When I have attempted to join myself to others by services, it proved an intellectual trick — no more. They eat your service like apples and leave you out. But love them, and they feel you and delight in you all the time.

Men are what their mothers made them.

The civilized man has built a coach but has lost the use of his feet.

We must be our own before we can be another's.

To different minds, the same world is a hell and a heaven.

The martyr cannot be dishonored. Every lash inflicted is a tongue of fame; every prison a more illustrious abode.

The machine unmakes the man. Now that the machine is so perfect, the engineer is nobody.

The selfish man suffers more from his selfishness than he from whom that selfishness withholds some important benefit.

All mankind loves a lover.

The reason why men do not obey us is because they see the mud at the bottom of our eye.

Man is timid and apologetic; he is no longer upright; he dares not say 'I think,' 'I am,' but quotes some saint or sage. He is ashamed before the blade of grass or the blowing rose. These roses under my window make no reference to former roses or to better ones.

Morality and Virtue

We gain the strength of the temptation we resist.

Every violation of truth is not only a sort of suicide in the liar, but is a stab at the health of human society.

It is very hard to be simple enough to be good.

The less a man thinks or knows about his virtues the better we like him.

We sell the thrones of angels for a short and turbulent pleasure.

Civilization depends on morality.

The virtue in most request is conformity.

Crime and punishment grow out of one stem. Punishment is a fruit that unsuspected ripens with the flower of the pleasure that concealed it.

The meaning of good and bad, of better and worse, is simply helping or hurting.

In failing circumstances no one can be relied on to keep their integrity.

The virtues of society are vices of the saint.

The terror of reform is the discovery that we must cast away our virtues, or what we have always esteemed such, into the same pit that has consumed our grosser vices.

You cannot do wrong without suffering wrong.

What is a weed? A plant whose virtues have not yet been discovered.

The only sin which we never forgive in each other is difference of opinion.

That which we call sin in others is experiment for us.

There is no den in the wide world to hide a rogue. Commit a crime and the earth is made of glass. Commit a crime, and it seems as if a coat of snow fell on the ground, such as reveals in the woods the track of every partridge and fox and squirrel and mole.

The only reward of virtue is virtue.

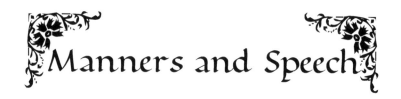

Manners and Speech

Good manners are made up of petty sacrifices.

We sometimes meet an original gentleman who, if manners had not existed, would have invented them.

Conversation is a game of circles.

Society is a masked ball where everyone hides his real character, and reveals it by hiding.

Life is not so short but that there is always time for courtesy.

The basis of good manners is self-reliance.

Conversation is an art in which a man has all mankind for his competitors, for it is that which all are practicing every day while they live.

No one is too big to be courteous, but some are too little.

The eloquent man is he who is no eloquent speaker but who is inwardly drunk with a certain belief.

Culture is one thing and varnish is another.

God may forgive sins, he said, but awkwardness has no forgiveness in heaven or earth.

Sincerity is the highest compliment you can pay.

Fine manners need the support of fine manners in others, and this is a gift interred only by the self.

Manners are the happy ways of doing things; each once a stroke of genius or of love, — now repeated and hardened into usage. They form at last a rich varnish, with which the routine of life is washed, and its details adorned.

Speech is power: speech is to persuade, to convert, to compel. It is to bring another out of his bad sense into your good sense.

'Tis a rule of manners to avoid exaggeration.

Wit makes its own welcome, and levels all distinctions. No dignity, no learning, no force of character, can make any stand against good wit.

Nothing is more vulgar than haste.

Education and Vocation

The secret in education lies in respecting the student.

The studious classes are their own victims: they are thin and pale, their feet are cold, their heads are hot, the night is without sleep, the day a fear of interruption — pallor, squalor, hunger and egotism.

A sage is the instructor of a hundred ages.

I pay the schoolmaster, but 'tis the schoolboys that educate my son.

I pronounce that young man happy who is content with having acquired the skill which he had aimed at, and waits willingly when the occasion of making it appreciated shall arrive, knowing well that it will not loiter.

One of the benefits of a college education is to show the boy its little avail.

My work is a game, a very serious game.

Each man has his own vocation; his talent is his call. There is one direction in which all space is open to him.

The crowning fortune of a man is to be born to some pursuit which finds him employment and happiness, whether it be to make baskets, or broadswords, or canals, or statues, or songs.

The first farmer was the first man, and all historic nobility rests on possession and use of land.

The man who can make hard things easy is the educator.

Criticism should not be querulous and wasting, all knife and root-puller, but guiding, instructive, inspiring.

Bad times have a scientific value. These are occasions a good learner would not miss.

We learn geology the morning after the earthquake.

All the great speakers were bad speakers at first.

There is no teaching until the pupil is brought into the same state or principle in which you are; a transfusion takes place; he is you, and you are he; there is a teaching; and by no unfriendly chance or bad company can he ever quite lose the benefit.

The years teach us much the days never knew.

When I was praised I lost my time, for instantly I turned around to look at the work I had thought slightly of, and that day I made nothing new.

Conversation is the laboratory and workshop of the student.

Universities are of course hostile to geniuses which, seeing and using ways of their own, discredit the routine: as churches and monasteries persecute youthful saints.

We are students of words: we are shut up in schools and colleges and recitation-rooms for ten or fifteen years, and come out at last with a bag of wind, a memory of words, and do not know a thing.

The wonder is always new that any sane man can be a sailor.

The sum of wisdom is, that the time is never lost that is devoted to work.

Be yourself; no base imitator of another, but your best self. There is something which you can do better than another. Listen to the inward voice and bravely obey that. Do the things at which you are great, not what you were never made for.

If a man's eye is on the eternal his intellect will grow.

Meek young man grow up in libraries believing it their duty to accept the views which Cicero, which Locke, which Bacon, have given, forgetful that Cicero, Locke and Bacon were only young men in libraries when they wrote these books. Hence instead of man thinking, we have the book-worm.

A boy who knows that a bully lives round the corner which he must pass on his daily way to school, is apt to take sinister views of streets and of school education.

The time your rival spends in dressing up his work for effect, hastily, and for the market, you spend in study and experiments towards real knowledge and efficiency... You have raised yourself into a higher school of art, and a few years will show the advantage of the real master over the short popularity of the showman.

Talent for talent's sake is a bauble and a show. Talent working with joy in the cause of universal truth lifts the possessor to a new power as a benefactor.

We must hold a man amenable to reason for the choice of his daily craft or profession. It is not an excuse any longer for his deeds that they are the custom of his trade. What business has he with an evil trade?

Knowledge exists to be imparted.

I suffer whenever I see that common sight of a parent or senior imposing his opinion and way of thinking and being on a young soul to which they are totally unfit. Cannot we let people be themselves and enjoy life in their own way? You are trying to make another you. One's enough.

Talent is commonly developed at the expense of character.

Every really able man, in whatever direction he work,— a man of large affairs, an inventor, a statesman, an orator, a poet, a painter,— if you talk sincerely with him, considers his work, however much admired, as far short of what it should be.

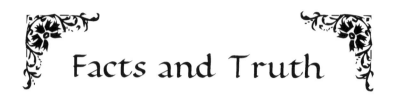

Facts and Truth

If a man will kick a fact out of the window, when he comes back he finds it again in the chimney corner.

Whatever games are played with us, we must play no games with ourselves, but deal in our privacy with the last honesty and truth.

The most dangerous thing is illusion.

The greatest homage we can pay truth is to use it.

You cannot see the mountain near.

The hues of the opal, the light of the diamond, are not to be seen if the eye is too near.

Truth is the property of no individual but is the treasure of all men.

God offers to every mind its choice between truth and repose.

Curiosity is lying in wait for every secret.

No facts are to me sacred; none are profane; I simply experiment, an endless seeker with no past at my back.

The highest compact we can make with our fellow is: 'Let there be truth between us two forevermore.'

Truth is the summit of being.

Emotions and Attitudes

We aim above the mark to hit the mark.

Some of your hurts you have cured, and the sharpest you still have survived, but what torments of grief you endured from evils which never arrived!

I know of no such unquestionable badge and ensign of a sovereign mind as that of tenacity of purpose.

Sympathy is a supporting atmosphere, and in it we unfold easily and well.

Insist upon yourself. Be original.

Imitation is suicide.

Enthusiasm is the leaping lightning, not to be measured by the horse- power of the understanding.

Patience and fortitude conquer all things.

Fear defeats more people than any other one thing in the world.

The eye is easily frightened.

Those who cannot tell what they desire or expect still sigh and struggle with indefinite thoughts and vast wishes.

Columbus discovered no isle or key so lonely as himself.

To fill the hour — that is happiness.

Judge of your natural character by what you do in your dreams.

We change, whether we like it or not.

One ought never to turn one's back on a threatened danger and try to run away from it. If you do that you will double the danger. But if you meet it promptly and without flinching you will reduce the danger by half. Never run away from anything. Never!

A good indignation brings out all one's powers.

Let me never fall into the vulgar mistake of dreaming that I am persecuted whenever I am contradicted.

A man makes inferiors his superiors by heat; self control is the rule.

Passion, though a bad regulator, is a powerful spring.

Whenever you are sincerely pleased you are nourished.

Little minds have little worries, big minds have no time for worries.

Beware what you set your heart upon, for it shall surely be yours.

Concentration is the secret of strength in politics, in war, in trade, in short in all the management of human affairs.

Discontent is want of self-reliance; it is infirmity of will.

The moment we indulge our affections the earth is metamorphosed, there is no winter and no night; all tragedies, all ennuis, vanish, all duties even.

When we quarrel, how we wish we had been blameless!

Nothing can bring you peace but yourself; nothing but the triumph of principles.

Seeing only what is fair, sipping only what is sweet... Leave the chaff, and take the wheat.

Nothing external to you has any power over you.

It is a happy talent to know how to play.

So of cheerfulness or a good temper, the more it is spent, the more it remains.

Happiness is a perfume which you cannot pour on someone without getting some on yourself.

A foolish consistency is the hobgoblin of little minds, adored by little statesmen and philosophers and divines.

Self-trust is the first secret of success, the belief that if you are here the authorities of the universe put you here, and for cause, or with some task strictly appointed you in your constitution,

Trust your instinct to the end, though you can render no reason.

Riding a horse is not a gentle hobby, to be picked up and laid down like a game of Solitaire. It is a grand passion.

Often a certain abdication of prudence and foresight is an element of success.

Cultivate the habit of being grateful for every good thing that comes to you, and to give thanks continuously. And because all things have contributed to your advancement, you should include all things in your gratitude.

Our strength grows out of our weakness.

The wise man in the storm prays to God not for safety from danger but for deliverance from fear.

Self-sacrifice is the real miracle out of which all the reported miracles grow.

I dip my pen in the blackest ink because I am not afraid of falling into my inkpot.

Nor count compartments of the floors, but mount to paradise by the stairway of surprise.

Fear always springs from ignorance.

A good intention clothes itself with sudden power.

War and Peace

Peace has its victories, but it takes a brave man to win them.

Peace cannot be achieved through violence; it can only be attained through understanding.

The god of victory is said to be one-handed, but peace gives victory on both sides.

Thoughts

Thought is the blossom; language the bud;
action the fruit behind it.

Common sense is genius dressed in its
working clothes.

*Our knowledge is the amassed thought
and experience of innumerable minds.*

If a man sits down to think, he is
immediately asked if he has a headache.

Our best thoughts come from others.

What your heart thinks is great, is great.
The soul's emphasis is always right.

Every thought which genius and piety throw into the world alters world.

Knowledge is knowing that we cannot know.

For every minute you are angry, you lose sixty seconds of happiness.

We are wiser than we know.

Nothing is at last sacred but the integrity of your own mind.

The soul of God is poured into the world through the thoughts of men.

Some thoughts always find us young, and keep us so. Such a thought is the love of the universal and eternal beauty.

What is the hardest thing in the world? To think.

We boast our emancipation from many superstitions; but if we have broken any idols it is through a transfer of idolatry.

Sow a thought and you reap an action; sow an act and you reap a habit; sow a habit and you reap a character; sow a character and you reap a destiny.

Stay at home in your mind. Don't recite other people's opinions. I hate quotations. Tell me what you know.

We are the prisoners of ideas.

It is a lesson which all history teaches wise man; to put trust in ideas and not in circumstances.

Beware when the great God lets loose a thinker on this planet.

To think is to act.

He presents me with what is always an acceptable gift who brings me news of a great thought before unknown. He enriches me without impoverishing himself.

There is no knowledge that is not power.

We lie in the lap of immense intelligence.

The invariable mark of wisdom is to see the miraculous in the common.

Thought is the blossom; language the bud; action the fruit behind it.

Fate then is a name for facts not yet passed under the fire of thought; for causes which are unpenetrated.

'Tis good-will makes intelligence.

If I cannot brag of knowing something, then I brag of not knowing it; at any rate, brag.

A chief event of life is the day in which we have encountered a mind that startled us.

Cunning is strength withheld.

God, Religion and Belief

Belief consists in accepting the affirmations of the soul; unbelief, in denying them.

'Tis the old secret of the gods that they come in low disguises.

We are born believing. A man bears beliefs as a tree bears apples.

The religion that is afraid of science dishonors God and commits suicide.

Religion is as effectually destroyed by bigotry as by indifference.

Our faith comes in moments, yet there is a depth in those brief moments which constrains us to ascribe more reality to them than to all other experiences.

The dice of God are always loaded.

All that I have seen teaches me to trust the Creator for all I have not seen.

There is a crack in everything God has made.

The fatal trait of the times is the divorce between religion and morality.

Like any other gift, the gift of grace can be yours only if you'll reach out and take it.

The growth of the intellect is spontaneous in every expansion. The mind that grows could not predict the times, the means, the mode of that spontaneity. God enters by a private door into every individual.

The disease with which the human mind now labors is want of faith.

The good rain, like a bad preacher, does not know when to leave off.

The faith that stands on authority is not faith.

As men's prayers are a disease of the will, so are their creeds a disease of the intellect.

The god of the cannibals will be a cannibal, of the crusaders a crusader, and of the merchants a merchant.

Alas for the unhappy man that is called to stand in the pulpit and not give the bread of life.

Let us be silent that we may hear the whispers of the gods.

Doing

Why should we be cowed by the name of Action?

Real action is in silent moments.

Act, if you like, but you do it at your peril. Men's actions are too strong for them. Show me a man who has acted and who has not been the victim and slave of his action.

Do the thing we fear, and the death of fear is certain.

You cannot do a kindness too soon, for you never know how soon it will be too late.

Ideas must work through the brains and the arms of good and brave men or they are no better than dreams.

That which builds is better than that which is built.

Do that which is assigned to you and you cannot hope too much or dare too much.

Skill to do comes of doing.

Always do what you are afraid to do.

We are taught by great actions that the universe is the property of every individual in it.

Enthusiasm is the mother of effort, and without it nothing great was ever achieved.

You are constantly invited to be what you are.

The best way to find yourself is to lose yourself in the service of others.

Go put your creed into your deed.

We do what we must, and call it by the best names.

Necessity does everything well.

None of us will ever accomplish anything excellent or commanding except when he listens to this whisper which is heard by him alone.

Each time we face our fear, we gain strength, courage and confidence in the doing.

All promise outruns performance.

Do what you know and perception is converted into character.

That which we persist in doing becomes easier to do, not that the nature of the thing has changed but that our power to do has increased.

Be true to your own act and congratulate yourself if you have done something strange and extravagant to break the monotony of a decorous age.

The ancestor of every action is a thought.

A man's action is only a picture book of his creed.

It is hard to go beyond your public. If they are satisfied with a cheap performance you will not easily arrive at better. If they know what is good and require it, you will aspire and burn until you achieve it.

Men talk as if victory were something fortunate. Work is victory.

Men achieve a certain greatness unawares when working to another aim.

See only that thou work, and thou canst not escape the reward.

Curses always recoil on the head of him who imprecates them. If you put a chain around the neck of a slave the other end fastens itself around your own.

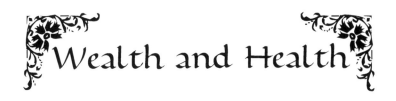

Wealth and Health

When you have worn out your shoes, the strength of the sole leather has passed into the fibre of your body. I measure your health by the number of shoes and hats and clothes you have worn out. He is the richest man who pays the largest debt to his shoemaker.

Give me health and a day, and I will make the pomp of emperors ridiculous.

Health is the condition of wisdom, and the sign is cheerfulness — an open and noble temper.

Without the rich heart, wealth is an ugly beggar.

Wealth is in applications of mind to nature; and the art of getting rich consists not in industry, much less in saving, but in a better order, in timeliness, in being at the right spot.

Can anything be so elegant as to have few wants and to serve them one's self?

Our expenses are all for conformity.

There is no prosperity, trade, art, city or great material wealth of any kind but if you trace it home you will find it rooted in a thought of some individual man.

Imagination is not a talent of some people but is the health of everyone.

Money often costs too much.

It is dainty to be sick, if you have leisure and convenience for it.

There are three wants which never can be satisfied: that of the rich who wants something more; that of the sick who wants something different; and that of the traveler who says anywhere but here.

All diseases run into one. Old age.

It requires a great deal of boldness and a great deal of caution to make a great fortune, and when you have, it requires ten times as much skill to keep it.

Pay every debt as if God wrote the bill.

It is always so pleasant to be generous, though very vexatious to pay debts.

Want is a growing giant whom the coat of Have was never large enough to cover.

No man acquires property without acquiring with it a little arithmetic also.

The first wealth is health.

Art, language and Literature

In art, the hand can never execute anything higher than the heart can inspire.

Fiction reveals truth that reality obscures.

It makes a great difference in the force of a sentence whether a man be behind it or no.

Art is a jealous mistress; and if a man have a genius for painting, poetry, music, architecture or philosophy, he makes a bad husband and an ill provider.

Life too near paralyses art.

The True Artist has the planet for his pedestal; the adventurer after many years of strife has nothing broader than his shoes.

Artists must be sacrificed to their art. Like the bees they must put their lives into the sting they give.

Our high respect for a well-read man is praise enough for literature.

Language is fossil poetry.

The imagination and the senses cannot be gratified at the same time.

Talent alone cannot make a writer. There must be a man behind the book; a personality which by birth and quality is pledged to the doctrines there set forth and which exists to see and state things so and not otherwise.

A man's library is a sort of harem.

Eloquence is the power to translate a truth into language perfectly intelligible to the person to whom you speak.

Music causes us to think eloquently.

We are as much informed of a writer's genius by what he selects as by what he originates.

Books are the best of things, well used; abused, among the worst. They are for nothing but to inspire. I had better never see a book than to be warped by its attraction clean out of my own orbit, and made a satellite instead of a system.

Some books leave us free and some books make us free.

I can find my biography in every fable that I read.

Music is the poor man's Parnassus.

The profit of books is according to the sensibility of the reader. The profoundest thought or passion sleeps as in a mine until an equal mind and heart finds and publishes it.

'Tis the good reader that makes the good book; a good head cannot read amiss, in every book he finds passages which seem confidences or asides hidden from all else and unmistakably meant for his ear.

People do not deserve to have good writings; they are so pleased with the bad.

The life of man is the true romance, which when it is valiantly conduced, will yield the imagination a higher joy than any fiction.

The torpid artist seeks inspiration at any cost, by virtue or by vice, by friend or by fiend, by prayer or by wine.

No book was ever written down by any but itself.

If we encounter a man of rare intellect we should ask him what books he reads.

Art and power will go on as they have done—will make day out of night, time out of space, and space out of time.

There is then creative reading as well as creative writing. When the mind is braced by labor and invention, the page of whatever book we read becomes luminous.

A work of art is an abstract or epitome of the world. It is the result or expression of nature, in miniature.

The Gothic cathedral is a blossoming in stone subdued by the insatiable demand of harmony in man. The mountain of granite blooms into an eternal flower, with the lightness and delicate finish as well as the aerial proportions and perspective of vegetable beauty.

Love of beauty is Taste. The creation of beauty is Art.

Language is a city to the building of which every human being brought a stone.

Each work of art excludes the world and concentrates on itself. For the time it is the only thing worth doing — to do just that; be it a sonnet, a statue, a landscape, an outline head of Caesar or an oration. Presently we return to the sight of another that globes itself into a whole as did the first, for example a beautiful garden; and nothing seems worth doing in life but laying out a garden.

The quality of the imagination is to flow and not to freeze.

The true poem is the poet's mind.

Proverbs, like the sacred books of each nation, are the sanctuary of the intuitions.

Science does not know its debt to imagination.

Genius borrows nobly. When Shakespeare is charged with debts to his authors, Landor replies, 'Yet he was more original than his originals. He breathed upon dead bodies and brought them into life.'

The conscious utterance of thought, by speech or action, to any end, is art.

There is no way to success in art but to take off your coat, grind paint, and work like a digger on the railroad all day and every day.

Be a little careful about your library. Do you foresee what you will do with it? Very little, to be sure. But the real question is what will it do with you? You will come here and get books that will open your eyes, and your ears, and your curiosity, and turn you inside out or outside in.

By necessity, by proclivity, and by delight, we all quote.

It has come to be practically a sort of rule in literature, that a man, having once shown himself capable of original writing, is entitled thenceforth to steal from the writings of others at discretion.

Every artist was first an amateur.

The lesson taught by the study of Greek and of Gothic art, of antique and of Pre-Raphaelite painting, was worth all the research,— namely, that all beauty must be organic; that outside embellishment is deformity.

In sculpture did ever anybody call the Apollo a fancy piece? Or say of the Laocoon how it might be made different? A masterpiece of art has in the mind a fixed place in the chain of being, as much as a plant or a crystal.

The production of a work of art throws a light upon the mystery of humanity.

Light is the first of painters. There is no object so foul that intense light will not make it beautiful.

Perpetual modernness is the measure of merit in every work of art.

Sculpture and painting have the effect of teaching us manners and abolishing hurry.

What is imagination? Only an arm or weapon of the interior energy; only the precursor of the reason.

World, State and Government

The less government we have the better.

Every reform was once a private opinion, and when it shall be a private opinion again it will solve the problem of the age.

The imbecility of men is always inviting the impudence of power.

An empire is an immense egotism.

Give no bounties; make equal laws; secure life and prosperity, and you need not give alms.

A man's wife has more power over him than the state has.

The President has paid dear for his White House. It has commonly cost him all his peace and the best of his manly attributes. To preserve for a short time so conspicuous an appearance before the world, he is content to eat dust before the real masters who stand erect behind the throne.

The only thing in the world of value is the active soul.

I am ashamed to think how easily we capitulate to badges and names, to large societies and dead institutions.

Good men must not obey the laws too well.

Nations have lost their old omnipotence; the patriotic tie does not hold. Nations are getting obsolete; we go and live where we will.

Wherever there is power there is age.

There is properly no history; only biography.

It is said that the world is in a state of bankruptcy, that the world owes the world more than the world can pay, and ought to go into chancery and be sold.

Every great and commanding movement in the annals of the world is due to the triumph of enthusiasm.

I do not see how a barbarous community and a civilized community can constitute a state. I think we must get rid of slavery or we must get rid of freedom.

We estimate the wisdom of nations by seeing what they did with their surplus capital.

The more reason, the less government.

No law can be sacred to me but that of my nature.

If you shoot at a king you must kill him.

'Tis pedantry to estimate nations by the census, or by square miles of land, or other than by their importance to the mind of the time.

The world always had the same bankrupt look to foregoing ages as to us.

Conservatism makes no poetry, breathes no prayer, has no invention; it is all memory. Reform has no gratitude, no prudence, no husbandry.

All history is a record of the power of minorities and of minorities of one.

The world is his who has the money to go over it.

As long as our civilization is essentially one of property, of fences, of exclusiveness, it will be mocked by delusions. Our riches will leave us sick; there will be bitterness in our laughter; and our wine will burn our mouth.

A nation never falls but by suicide.

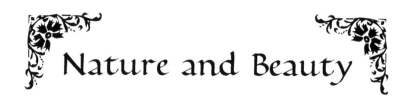

Nature and Beauty

To the dull mind all nature is leaden. To the illumined mind the whole world burns and sparkles with light.

Earth laughs in flowers.

There is no beautifier of complexion, or form, or behavior, like the wish to scatter joy and not pain around us.

Though we travel the world over to find the beautiful, we must carry it with us or we find it not.

Beauty without grace is the hook without the bait.

Nature is too thin a screen; the glory of the omnipresent God bursts through everywhere.

The man who has seen the rising moon break out of the clouds at midnight has been present like an archangel at the creation of light and of the world.

Beauty is the mark God sets upon virtue. Every natural action is graceful. Every heroic act is also decent and causes the place and the bystanders to shine.

A man is related to all nature.

A life in harmony with nature, the love of truth and virtue, will purge the eyes to understanding her text.

One of the most wonderful things in nature is a glance of the eye; it transcends speech; it is the bodily symbol of identity.

The rich mind lies in the sun and sleeps and is Nature.

To speak truly, few adult persons can see nature. Most persons do not see the sun. At least they have a very superficial seeing. The sun illuminates only the eye of the man, but shines into the eye and heart of the child.

Nature is full of freaks and now puts an old head on young shoulders and then takes a young heart beating under fourscore winters.

Flowers are a proud assertion that a ray of beauty out-values all the utilities of the world.

Plants are the young of the world, vessels of health and vigor; but they grope ever upward towards consciousness; the trees are imperfect men, and seem to bemoan their imprisonment, rooted in the ground.

Everything in Nature contains all the powers of Nature. Everything is made of hidden stuff.

If the stars should appear one night in a thousand years, how would men believe and adore; and preserve for many generations the remembrance of the city of God which had been shown!

Beauty is the pilot of the young soul.

Nature is an endless combination and repetition of a very few laws. She hums the old well-known air through innumerable variations.

Nature, she pardons no mistakes. Her yea is yea, and her nay, nay.

Nothing is rich but the inexhaustible wealth of nature. She shows us only surfaces, but she is a million fathoms deep.

Nature magically suits a man to his fortunes, by making them the fruit of his character.

Few people know how to take a walk. The qualifications are endurance, plain clothes, old shoes, an eye for nature, good humor, vast curiosity, good speech, good silence and nothing too much.

Chide me not, laborious band! for the idle flowers I brought; every aster in my hand goes home loaded with a thought.

We live by our imagination, our admirations, and our sentiments.

Greatness and Heroism

Coffee is good for talent but genius wants prayer.

To be great is to be misunderstood.

Great people are they who see that spiritual is stronger than any material force, that thoughts rule the world.

A great man stands on God. A small man on a great man.

Not he is great who can alter matter, but he who can alter my state of mind.

The bigger they are, the further they have to fall.

The charm of the best courages is that they are inventions, inspirations, flashes of genius.

Great hearts steadily send forth the secret forces that incessantly draw great events.

When Nature has work to be done, she creates a genius to do it.

Self-trust is the essence of heroism.

Big jobs usually go to the men who prove their ability to outgrow small ones.

The hearing ear is always found close to the speaking tongue; and no genius can often utter anything which is not invited and gladly entertained by men around him.

No great man ever complains of want of opportunity.

With consistency a great soul has simply nothing to do. He may as well concern himself with his shadow on the wall. Speak what you think now in hard words and to-morrow speak what to-morrow thinks in hard words again, though it contradict every thing you said to-day.

Accept your genius and say what you think.

His heart was as great as the world, but there was no room in it to hold the memory of a wrong.

The silence that accepts merit as the most natural thing in the world is the highest applause.

There is no true orator who is not a hero.

Works of the intellect are great only by comparison with each other.

Great geniuses have the shortest biographies.

Courage consists in equality to the problem before us.

A hero is no braver than an ordinary man, but he is braver five minutes longer.

Half a man's wisdom goes with his courage.

What a new face courage puts on everything!

Every man has his own courage, and is betrayed because he seeks in himself the courage of other persons.

A great part of courage is the courage of having done the thing before.

He is great who is what he is from nature and who never reminds us of others.

Solitude, the safeguard of mediocrity, is to genius the stern friend.

Conversation enriches the understanding;
but solitude is the school of genius.

The essence of greatness is the perception
that virtue is enough.

When a resolute young fellow steps up to
the great bully the world and takes him
boldly by the beard, he is often surprised to
find it comes off in his hand, and that it was
only tied on to scare away the timid
adventurers.

Heroism feels and never reasons and
therefore is always right.

Whatever you do you need courage.

The search after the great men is the dream
of youth, and the most serious occupation of
manhood.

Nature never sends a great man into the
planet without confiding the secret to
another soul.

The characteristic of genuine heroism is its persistency. All men have wandering impulses, fits and starts of generosity. But when you have resolved to be great, abide by yourself and do not weakly try to reconcile yourself with the world. The heroic cannot be the common nor the common the heroic.

The greatest genius is the most indebted person.

The greatest man in history was the poorest.

Immortality will come to such as are fit for it, and he who would be a great soul in future must be a great soul now.

The first thing a great person does is make us realize the insignificance of circumstance.

The measure of a great leader is their success in bringing everyone around to their opinion twenty years later.

Valor consists in the power of self-recovery.

All history is but the lengthened shadow of a great man.

Courage charms us because it indicates that a man loves an idea better than all things in the world, that he is thinking neither of his bed nor his dinner nor his money, but will venture all to put in act the invisible thought of his mind.

A great man is always willing to be little.

Spartans, stoics, heroes, saints and gods use short and positive speech.

There is always safety in valor.

Character is higher than intellect. A great soul will be strong to live as well as think.

In every work of genius we recognize our own rejected thoughts; they come back to us with a certain alienated majesty.

A man of genius is privileged only as far as he is genius. His dullness is as insupportable as any other dullness.

He is great who confers the most benefits.

It is easy in the world to live after the world's opinion; it is easy in solitude after our own; but the great man is he who in the midst of the crowd keeps with perfect sweetness the independence of solitude.

To believe your own thought, to believe that what is true for you in your private heart is true for all men — that is genius.

Every hero becomes a bore at last.

Note from the Publisher

If you enjoyed this quote collection, you are sure to enjoy its companion volumes:

Inspiration & Wisdom from the Pen of George Eliot

With a touch both loving and wise, George Eliot wrote of many things. But it is her unique insight into human character for which she is valued above all. When reading any one of her great literary masterpieces, the reader is arrested from time to time by some sentence, metaphor or paragraph which sheds astonishing new light on a part of ourselves, the world, or the human condition. We stop, reread it, ponder on its genius and beauty. It is these gems which have been gathered from the great breadth of Eliot's work and are here presented in one concise book. Words on love, marriage, friendship, life, character, virtue, and many more topics, fill these pages. Few will close it without picking up some new pearls to add to their store of wisdom.

Odelia Floris

Inspiration
&
Wisdom
from the pen of
George Eliot

Over 250 Quotes

Available in paperback for just $7.99 USD.
Get it on Amazon.com today!

The Complete Poems of Ralph Waldo Emerson

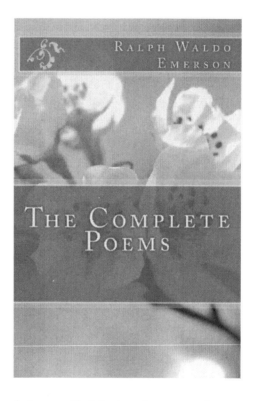

This book is available on Amazon in paperback for just $13.99 USD.

And lastly, please take a few minutes to leave a brief review on Amazon. Authors and publishers are always extremely grateful to receive them. Earnest Acorn Books would love to have yours!